GRACE AND GRATITUDE

A 40-DAY THANKSGIVING MEDITATION

CHARLES A. BARRETT

GRACE AND GRATITUDE

A 40-DAY THANKSGIVING MEDITATION

Grace and Gratitude: A 40-Day Thanksgiving Meditation

Published by

CAB Publishing Company, LLC

PO Box 1108

Leesburg, Virginia 20177

ISBN-13: 978-1-7350264-1-1

CONTENTS

ABOUT GRACE AND GRATITUDE

2020. A year like no other. A year that seems to be a drama or suspense-filled horror story with one unexpected plot twist after another. To say that it has been difficult is an understatement. Despite all of the positive affirmations that were made as we approached 2020, from seeing clearly or perfectly to everything coming into focus, the last few months have not been what we expected. In fact, if we knew what was on the other side of January 1, many of us would have opted to remain in 2019.

A global pandemic of epic proportions, the novel corona virus, also known as COVID-19, has affected people from all walks of life. While some lost jobs and financial security, others unexpectedly said goodbye to life-long friends and loved ones. With the constant recurrence of death, whether COVID related or otherwise, it's nearly impossible to casually scroll through our social media feeds without being inundated with scores of RIP tributes, almost to the point of becoming numb. With families devastated and economies decimated, chronic uncertainty perpetuates fear and anxiety.

And if COVID wasn't enough to overwhelm the world, social injustice as a consequence of systemic racism continues to rear its head through the senseless killings and mistreatment of unarmed individuals, particularly Black people living in the United States. Whether Breonna Taylor in Kentucky, Ahmaud Auberry in Georgia, George Floyd in Minnesota, or those whose names we don't know, civil unrest and political tensions exacerbated an already stressed citizenry during this complicated time in world history. From the turbulence of demonstrations for civil rights that are reminiscent of the 1960s, to political divisiveness and economic peril, you name it, 2020 has it.

But in spite of these things, and albeit counterintuitive due to how much life has changed, we still have a lot for which we can be thankful. In fact, I am reminded of these words recorded in the 17th and 18th verses of Habakkuk chapter 3:

Even though the fig trees have no blossoms, and there are no grapes on the vines;

even though the olive crop fails, and the fields lie empty and barren; even though

the flocks die in the fields, and the cattle barns are empty, yet I will rejoice in the

LORD! I will be joyful in the God of my salvation!

Despite wondering if we would make it this far, here we are. Amidst worrying about providing for ourselves, and juggling additional responsibilities for friends, family members, neighbors, and coworkers, we're still here. Although students were saddened because they couldn't finish the school year in face-to-face settings, and some endured the disappointment of not experiencing milestone events to celebrate their years of dedication and hard work, God is still good, and we are grateful.

Without denying how challenging this year continues to be, or the range of emotions that we are feeling, *Grace and Gratitude: A 40-Day Thanksgiving Meditation* is a collection of inspirational readings that centers our hearts and minds on being thankful and encourages you, the reader, with the hope that better days are ahead. For 40 days, I invite you to spend a few moments in quiet meditation reading a short passage of scripture, reflecting on the thought for the day, and writing a few notes that are important for you to remember. Depending on the day, your notes will take different forms. Sometimes they will be simple, yet significant things that you recall God doing for you or your loved ones. At other times they will be ideas that come to you after reading and reflecting. Whether personally encouraging sentiments that you don't want to forget, or ways that you can continue growing as a friend, sibling, spouse, employer, student, or leader, record and revisit them throughout the year.

As you read, reflect, and remember, know that I am thankful for you and always praying for you.

DEDICATION

*To the more than 600 individuals who have subscribed
to receive a daily text message from me, thank you.
I am grateful for the opportunity to encourage you
and speak into your lives.*

DAY 1

INVISIBLE BLESSINGS

God saved you by his grace when you believed.
And you can't take credit for this; it is a gift from God.
Salvation is not a reward for the good things we have done, so none of us can boast about it.

Ephesians 2: 8-9

The holiday season has always been one of my most favorite times of the year. Traditionally beginning with Thanksgiving, it's a wonderful time to think about everything that we have. Quite naturally, tangible objects come to mind—a place to live, food to eat, clothes to wear, money in the bank (regardless if it seems to be enough), and a host of other items that help to make life more comfortable and convenient. But as we're thinking about and thanking God for these blessings, we should also remember something that we often cannot see: grace. A lot can be said about this enduring quality of who God is and that is demonstrated in immeasurable ways; but a few things come to mind. It's God's patience with us. It's God providing for our needs. It's God's ability to restore us after there's been a breach in relationship. It's God's unconditional acceptance of us, despite what we've done. And perhaps most of all, it's God's everlasting love for us—one that never runs out. Although uncertainty abounds, grace abounds even more. And having been the recipients of such grace, let's extend the same to others.

Thanksgiving prompts us to reflect on our many blessings.
During this season, let's be thankful for the generous gift of grace that God has freely given to us.

WORK LESS, RECEIVE MORE

"For God loved the world so much that he gave his one and only Son,
so that everyone who believes in him will not perish but have eternal life."

John 3: 16

Since we were little children, many of us have been taught that hard work pays off. And while there is some truth to this, it can also lead to developing an unhealthy work ethic. In other words, we work more, in order to earn more, so that we can buy more. This, however, is not God's plan for us. Life is more than working to acquire earthly possessions. Life is also about becoming more comfortable with receiving. Consider these questions: how balanced is my lifestyle? Am I consumed with doing more in order to have more? How uncomfortable am I with receiving from others? Do I accept God's unconditional love for me? Starting today, let's unlearn unhealthy ways of living by readjusting our mindset to trust the unfailing love of God more than our own efforts.

Ephesians 2: 8-9 and John 3: 16 are not only examples of how much God loves us, but such love is not predicated on our actions. Receive the gift of God's love.

DAY 3

BLESSED TO BE A BLESSING

'For I was hungry, and you fed me. I was thirsty, and you gave me a drink. I was a stranger, and you invited me into your home. I was naked, and you gave me clothing. I was sick, and you cared for me. I was in prison, and you visited me.' "Then these righteous ones will reply, 'Lord, when did we ever see you hungry and feed you? Or thirsty and give you something to drink? Or a stranger and show you hospitality? Or naked and give you cloth- ing? When did we ever see you sick or in prison and visit you?' "And the King will say, 'I tell you the truth, when you did it to one of the least of these my brothers and sisters, you were doing it to me!'"

Matthew 25: 35-40

It is inaccurate to think that God takes care of everything. Yes, God is omnipotent; but because God is all powerful does not mean that God always uses such power to right the wrongs of the world. In fact, not only is restraint one of the best indicators of power, influence, or strength, but God is revealed through people—you and me. It is the everyday actions of feeding people, giving them something to drink, providing them with clothes to wear, caring for our neighbors when they are sick, and visiting those who are alone and lonely that not only demonstrate that God is real, but that God lives in us. In other words, we have been blessed to be a blessing. And because we have, others should never be without. But more than helping those in need, giving to those who can't give anything to us in return is the best way to show the love of God. Having been blessed to be a blessing, how can you bless someone today?

Because of grace, God freely and generously blesses us.
How can we voluntarily give to others in the same manner that God has blessed us?

DAY 4

RESTORATION

"So he returned home to his father. And while he was still a long way off, his father saw him coming. Filled with love and compassion, he ran to his son, embraced him, and kissed him. His son said to him, 'Father, I have sinned against both heaven and you, and I am no longer worthy of being called your son.' But his father said to the servants, 'Quick! Bring the finest robe in the house and put it on him. Get a ring for his finger and sandals for his feet. And kill the calf we have been fattening. We must celebrate with a feast, for this son of mine was dead and has now returned to life. He was lost, but now he is found.' So the party began."

Luke 15: 20-24

Being a fan of Home and Garden Television (HGTV), I have learned that renovating and remodeling homes is hard work. In virtually all instances, these projects require significant investments of time, money, and sweat equity. And while newly constructed homes have their appeal, some of my favorite episodes are those that have chronicled the restoration of abandoned and seemingly worthless properties. As difficult as it was, especially problem solving the almost inevitable unexpected complications that happen along the way, the end result is always worth it. Although the portion of the parable that is presented above offers a positive perspective on restoration, it's also a process. But just like vintage homes that are filled with character from centuries past, the restoration of relationships is worth it because of the inherent value of people. Despite the son being away from his father, there was more worth saving than abandoning. And although the son enjoyed a new beginning when he returned home, this didn't require him to start from the beginning. The same can happen for you and your relationships.

Be encouraged: grace restores. After making mistakes, we don't have to start over because God allows us to continue growing from where we were. Read Luke 15: 11-32.

DAY 5

IN HOT PURSUIT

"If a man has a hundred sheep and one of them wanders away, what will he do?
Won't he leave the ninety-nine others on the hills and go out to search for the one that is lost?
And if he finds it, I tell you the truth, he will rejoice over it more than over the ninety-nine that
didn't wander away! In the same way, it is not my heavenly Father's will
that even one of these little ones should perish."

Matthew 18: 12-14

Of all the qualities that are associated with love, two are often overlooked, or at least understated. First, love is intentional. Next, love is inconvenient. Although we talk about falling in love, this is fundamentally not possible because loving someone is a conscious decision. And having decided to love someone, it requires consistency in our actions that are not always easy. For those who love their children, if they wander away, what would you do? For those in romantic relationships, if your significant other or spouse frantically calls you because they are lost, what would you do? The intentional quality of love leads us to do for others at the most inconvenient times. If it's early in the morning, love says I'm on my way to meet you. If it's late at night, love says I'm coming to find you. But most of all, love is personal: giving us exactly what we need when we need it.

God's enduring love for us will never allow what we've done to stand in the way of faithfully and unconditionally pursuing an authentic relationship with us.

TWO QUESTIONS

"God blesses those who work for peace, for they will be called the children of God."

Matthew 5: 9

At some point in our lives, we must ask ourselves two questions. *Do I want to be right?* Or, *do I want to live in peace?* Although both of these can happen in the same situation, it's not always possible. Even in my own life, there have been times in which proving a point was more important than anything. Ultimately, however, it wasn't worth the time or frustration. It's true: life really is short. And because life is short, we need to enjoy as much peace as possible. Whatever it is that is infringing upon your peace of mind—your ability to sleep, rest, think clearly—I encourage you to take the necessary steps to settle the dispute. Make the phone call. Write the letter. Meet and talk. Or, resolve the situation for yourself and begin the process of working through your hurt, disappointment, and pain. Will these steps require effort? Yes. Will they always be easy? No. Will it be worth it? Absolutely. Will God give you strength? Every single time.

Some of us have relationships that need to be reconciled. Rather than holding grudges, let's actively restore others in the same manner that God restores us.

FAITH, VISION, AND BECOMING

"You don't have enough faith," Jesus told them. *"I tell you the truth, if you had faith even as small as a mustard seed, you could say to this mountain, 'Move from here to there,' and it would move. Nothing would be impossible."*

Matthew 17: 20

Vision is more than what we see, but what can be seen. More than what is, it's what can be. In some ways, vision is akin to faith and is more important and predictive of our success than skills, training, competence, or even experience. Like faith, vision inspires and motivates us to work through the temporary discomfort of the present knowing that there is more for us in the future. Vision is what empowers us when we're tired and encourages us when we feel like giving up. You are more than what you see today. And every day you are growing into the person that God has destined you to be. Be encouraged. You are becoming.

*Because grace unconditionally accepts, it sees the potential of who we are becoming
rather than who we are in our current stage of development. Be encouraged.*

DAY 8

GENUINE LOVE, AUTHENTIC RELATIONSHIP

Love is patient and kind. Love is not jealous or boastful or proud or rude. It does not demand its own way. It is not irritable, and it keeps no record of being wronged. It does not rejoice about injustice but rejoices whenever the truth wins out. Love never gives up, never loses faith, is always hopeful, and endures through every circumstance.

1 Corinthians 13: 4-7

Central to the human condition is the need for authentic connection and genuine relationship. But have you ever limited what you told certain people because you feared that they would judge you or look at you differently? Whether children hiding important things about themselves from their parents, or spouses keeping parts of their lives from one another, it's far from what God intends for our relationships. If you've never experienced it, this is my prayer for you: that you would meet at least one person who genuinely loves and cares about you. And despite knowing everything about you, their love, commitment, and concern for you never changes. When it comes your way, receive it. Trust it. Embrace it. It's freeing and you deserve it.

Say this out loud: *Despite knowing everything about me, God will never condemn, judge, or reject me. God genuinely loves, values, and accepts me.*

THE GOD OF A SECOND CHANCE

Once again you will have compassion on us.
You will trample our sins under your feet and throw them into the depths of the ocean!

Micah 7: 19

For years I've wrestled with the idea that God is the God of a second chance rather than being the God of another chance. Quite honestly, because God has given me more than a second chance in many areas of my life, wouldn't the God of another chance be technically correct? After much contemplation, I was reminded of the verse above and why God is always the God of a second chance. If we believe that God is the God of another chance, it suggests that God is tracking (e.g., remembering) every instance in which we've done wrong. It's almost as if God is begrudgingly giving us another chance to make a better decision. The God of a second chance, however, truly captures how God loves us and responds to us whenever we sin: God throws our sins into the depths of the sea. After we make mistakes and acknowledge them, it's as if they never happened. And when we make the same mistake, it's as if it's our first time. Because the other mistakes don't matter and the other missteps have been forgotten, we are always on our second chance with God.

When God forgives, God also forgets. So, if God can look beyond what we've done, and isn't dwelling on our past, we owe ourselves and others the same compassion.

DAY 10

THE INFINITE DEPTHS OF GOD'S LOVE

And I am convinced that nothing can separate us from God's love.
Neither death nor life, neither angels nor demons, neither our fears for today nor our worries
about tomorrow—not even the powers of hell can separate us from God's love.
No power in the sky above or in the earth below—indeed, nothing in all creation will ever be
able to separate us from the love of God that is revealed in Christ Jesus our Lord.

Romans 8: 38-39

Human intellect cannot fully grasp the concept of infinity. Imagine forever, which is a very long time. And at the end of forever, which is a very, very, very long time, forever has only just begun. I know it's lacking, but that's the best I can do to explain infinity—an endless number of forevers or infinite forevers. In the same manner, we can't truly fathom how expansive God's love is for us. Like forever and infinity, the end of those are only the beginning of God's love. God loves us so deeply, so fully, so completely, so endlessly because God has an everlasting, bottomless supply of love. Because God is love[1], God can never run out of God

---

Today, be encouraged knowing that grace is everlasting.
In other words, it is eternal, never runs out, and is as infinite as God's love for us.

DAY 11

IT'S ALL GOOD

Even though the fig trees have no blossoms, and there are no grapes on the vines; even though the olive crop fails, and the fields lie empty and barren; even though the flocks die in the fields, and the cattle barns are empty, yet I will rejoice in the LORD!
I will be joyful in the God of my salvation!

Habakkuk 3: 17-18

It has been said that every cloud has a silver lining. Similarly, life's challenges are often punctuated with something that is unexpectedly positive. As I'm writing this meditation, I don't want to overlook the pain and suffering that is the reality for many individuals. Being told to "look on the bright side" or "things could be worse" is not helpful and dismissive of what many are going through. As a psychologist, I've learned that it is okay for people to feel the range of emotions that are connected to the human experience. Disappointment. Sadness. Anger. Frustration. All of these are real and legitimate. The encouragement, however, is found in our ability to shift our perspective. In other words, although my circumstances are real, but less than ideal, God is also real. Although there is a lot going on around me, because God is real, I always have something for which I can be thankful. Challenging times and the goodness of God are not mutually exclusive. My situation may change, but God never changes. And because God never changes, I choose to shift my perspective by focusing on God's immutable qualities.

Being thankful isn't only about what we have but how we think. An attitude of gratitude ensures that we will always have something for which we can be thankful.

DAY 12

GOD IS ALWAYS AHEAD OF US

"Only I can tell you the future before it even happens..."
Isaiah 46: 10

There are so many things that I absolutely love about God. In the recent past, I have developed a deeper appreciation for how God truly knows the end from the beginning. As the Alpha and Omega[2], the first and last letters of the Greek alphabet, only God stands at the beginning of something and is simultaneously at the end of it. After recalling numerous occasions when God divinely orchestrated and resolved situations for me, I have been known to recite this phrase: *God is always ahead of us.* Whatever you need, whether right now or in the future, God has already provided it. And if God did it before, God can certainly do it again.

---

2   *"I am the Alpha and the Omega, the First and the Last, the Beginning and the End."* Revelation 22: 13. The Holy Bible, New Living Translation. Copyright © 1996, 2004, 2007 by Tyndale House Foundation. Used by permission of Tyndale House Publishers, Inc., Carol Stream, Illinois 60188. All rights reserved.

Although we should tell God how we feel, God knows everything before we say anything.
Today we can be grateful that God loves us and anticipates what we need.

YOU CAN'T BEAT GOD GIVING

"Give, and you will receive. Your gift will return to you in full—pressed down,
shaken together to make room for more, running over, and poured into your lap.
The amount you give will determine the amount you get back."

Luke 6: 38

You can't beat God giving

No matter how you try

And just as sure as you are living

And the Lord is in heaven on high

The more you give, the more He gives to you

But keep on giving because it's really true

That you can't beat God giving

No matter how you try[3]

Written by Doris Akers (d. 1995), these hymn lyrics are a powerful reminder that we can never give more than what God will return to us. In fact, it's a universal principle: giving makes room for more. And although our motivation to give is not to receive, as long as we're giving, we will never be without.

---

[3]   Akers, Doris. (1958). *You Can't Beat God Giving.*

Thanksgiving is as much about being thankful as it is about giving.
So, while we're thankful, let's always remember to give generously to those who are in need.

DAY 14

THE PRELUDE TO A MIRACLE

"There's a young boy here with five barley loaves and two fish. But what good is that with this huge crowd?" "Tell everyone to sit down," Jesus said. So they all sat down on the grassy slopes. (The men alone numbered about 5,000.) Then Jesus took the loaves, gave thanks to God, and distributed them to the people. Afterward he did the same with the fish. And they all ate as much as they wanted. After everyone was full, Jesus told his disciples, "Now gather the leftovers, so that nothing is wasted." So they picked up the pieces and filled twelve baskets with scraps left by the people who had eaten from the five barley loaves.

John 6: 9-13

One of the greatest miracles recorded in scripture was the feeding of more than five thousand people with a little boy's lunch. But what's often overlooked is how this was possible. It's a simple premise that I know can work in our lives as well. Before the bread and fish were distributed to the crowd of men, women, and children, Jesus said thank you. And what seemed like an insignificant gesture, was actually the catalyst for the miracle. Whenever we acknowledge that we are not the source of what we have, God trusts us with more. Whenever we recognize that God empowers and equips us to do great things, amazing things will happen. Saying thank you not only puts things in proper perspective but it's often the prelude to a miracle.

Being thankful is a prelude to giving. When we think that we don't have much to offer,
it helps us to see how blessed we are and what we can do to help others.

DAY 15

THINKING OF YOU

Every time I think of you, I give thanks to my God.

Philippians 1: 3

Have you ever received a call from someone who didn't want anything from you? Ever opened a *thinking about you* card from someone that you haven't heard from in a while? Perhaps you received an email or text message from a friend who simply wanted to say hello. How did these acts of kindness make you feel? Did they put a smile on your face? If they did, how about doing the same for someone else today? Make the telephone call. Mail the card. Write the email. Send the text message. Visit a neighbor. As much as God loves us, human connection is also necessary. Do it today. I guarantee that you will brighten someone's day.

Today I am praying that you feel how deeply someone loves you and appreciates you.
Be encouraged.

NOTHING LASTS FOREVER

...weeping may last through the night, but joy comes with the morning.

Psalm 30: 5

I know it's dark, but morning is coming. I know that death seems to be surrounding you, but there is life after this. I know that you're tired, but you will receive strength. I know that you're disappointed, but ultimate satisfaction will eventually be yours. All of these things are hard. But in the words of my friend Amber Boykin, *we can endure hard things if we know that they don't last forever.*[4]

---

4   Inspired by a Facebook post by Amber Boykin.

More than a day, Thanksgiving is every day.
Today I am thankful that my past experiences did not destroy me, but they helped to develop me.

DAY 17

IT WON'T WORK

"But in that coming day no weapon turned against you will succeed. You will silence every voice raised up to accuse you. These benefits are enjoyed by the servants of the LORD; their vindication will come from me. I, the LORD, have spoken!"

Isaiah 54: 17

For the myriad situations that you are facing today, be encouraged with these three words: it won't work. For those who know that people are trying to sabotage what you're building, it won't work. For those who are being misrepresented and falsely accused, it won't work. For those who are being unfairly scrutinized and criticized, it won't work. Whatever people are using to distract or discourage you, it won't work.

More than a day, Thanksgiving is a season. Today I'm thankful that although there are those who may not like me, they won't triumph over me.

DAY 18

I AM

"But Moses protested, "If I go to the people of Israel and tell them, 'The God of your ancestors has sent me to you,' they will ask me, 'What is his name?' Then what should I tell them?" God replied to Moses, "I AM WHO I AM. Say this to the people of Israel: I AM has sent me to you."

Exodus 3: 13-14

For those of us who have multiple names—first names, middle names, maiden names, nicknames, and last names—we still have far fewer than God. And as we are known by different names to different people, each name that God has represents a unique way in which God is known. In other words, one name is not enough. But if we had to use one name to capture everything that God is, I AM is most fitting. As the I AM, God is whatever we need. Lost and in need of direction? I AM is a shepherd. Worried about our physical, emotional, or mental health? I AM is a healer. In need of provision? I AM is a provider. God is whatever and everything we need God to be.

Today I am thankful that God is a Way Maker, Miracle Worker, Promise Keeper, and Light in Darkness.[5] In other words, God is God enough to be whatever I need.

---

5   Okoro, Osinachi. "Way Maker." Better Word, Integrity Music, 2018.

IN ALL THINGS I GIVE YOU THANKS

Be thankful in all circumstances, for this is God's will for you who belong to Christ Jesus.

1 Thessalonians 5: 18

As real as feelings are, they require balance. Yes, we should allow ourselves to feel the full range of our emotions; but we must also be careful to not be controlled by our emotions. While they are legitimate, feelings are also fleeting. And because they are not final, feelings must be balanced with discipline. In other words, even when we don't feel like being thankful, we maintain an attitude of gratitude. Like exercise, this is not always convenient. But the more we do it, the easier it becomes. Remember: thanksgiving is more than what we do; it's how we think.

Because gratitude is an attitude, today I'm thankful that what I feel doesn't determine how I think. Although it's not always easy, in all things I give thanks.

WE ARE NEVER ALONE

The LORD of Heaven's Armies is here among us; the God of Israel is our fortress.

Psalm 46: 11

Knowing that we don't have to experience difficult situations by ourselves is sometimes all we need to get through our most challenging moments. More than answers to our questions, or a quick fix to what is bothering us, we want to know that someone is walking with us through our darkest valleys. The bookends for the verses that comprise the 46th Psalm, we rest in the comfort and confidence that God is *always ready to help in times of trouble* (v. 1) and is *here among us* (v. 11).

Despite not having eveything we want, Thanksgiving is about celebrating God's grace and strength being with us—carrying us when we can't sustain ourselves.

DAY 21

PURPOSE IS A NEW PRESCRIPTION

For we are God's masterpiece, He has created us anew in Christ Jesus,
so we can do the good things he planned for us long ago.

Ephesians 2: 10

Without purpose, life would be meaningless. For those who must wear eyeglasses or contact lenses, each person's prescription is unique to their vision needs. Not too long ago, I went to the optometrist for a routine eye exam. As she showed me letters of varying sizes, although I was able to read all of the lines, using my old prescription some of them were blurry or less clear. By the end of the visit, the doctor adjusted my prescription, which brought everything into focus with relative ease. This is what purpose does for us: it makes everything clearer—sharper. Everyone has a purpose—not only what we are meant to do, but also why we exist. Purpose gives us the extra push to get out of bed knowing that there is something that we are destined to accomplish. Do you know your purpose? If you don't, ask God to reveal it to you. But also think about what you enjoy doing. Think about what brings you total satisfaction. What are you drawn to naturally? What can you not do? I guarantee it: wrapped up in these things is your purpose—your reason for living.

Today I'm thankful that because my life has purpose, I don't have to search for ways to fulfill my purpose: opportunities to live on and for purpose find me.

DAY 22

A FORMULA FOR SUCCESS

Work hard so you can present yourself to God and receive his approval. Be a good worker, one who does not need to be ashamed and who correctly explains the word of truth.

2 Timothy 2: 15

At the risk of oversimplifying life, and not fully appreciating the complexity of everyone's respective journey, there are three central elements to success. First, we need to be aware of our gifts. Like purpose, everyone has a gift—something that we do well, almost naturally and with little effort. For some it's having the right words to encourage people. For others it's teaching, organizing events, or even carpentry—the ability to see what can be and effectively building it for others to enjoy. Next, is preparation. Although we're gifted, we must also study to develop and continually hone our skills. Even gifted musicians discipline themselves by practicing, participating in years of lessons, and earning advanced degrees in order to understand all of the nuances of their gift. Last, is opportunity—the chance to use our gifts and fulfill the purpose for which we were created. But if one of these is missing, success is less likely. We can be gifted but unprepared for an opportunity that presents itself. We can be gifted but never have a chance to demonstrate what we've prepared ourselves to do. Gifting + Preparation + Opportunity = Success.

52

Today we can be thankful that God has not only given us talent, but we have also been equipped with the tools that talent needs for us to fulfill our purpose.

DAY 23

I CAN SEE CLEARLY NOW

For our present troubles are small and won't last very long.   Yet they produce for us a glory that vastly outweighs them and will last forever! So we don't look at the troubles we can see now; rather, we fix our gaze on things that cannot be seen.   For the things we see now will soon be gone, but the things we cannot see will last forever.

2 Corinthians 4: 17-18

Perspective is important. The manner in which we view a situation has tremendous influence over how we experience it. When we face a challenging circumstance, especially something that is beyond our control, what is our outlook on the situation? Is this something to frustrate me? Or, could there be another reason for what is happening in my life? Without denying what you're going through, think about how this is not only developing you in certain ways, but also positioning you to help someone else. God doesn't create everything; but God can certainly use anything to help us grow and fulfill our purpose.

Today I am thankful that I see it: what was trying to frustrate me was actually meant to focus me on what really matters: the fact that God is always with me.

DAY 24

CELEBRATE THE SMALL THINGS

Then God said, "Let there be light," and there was light. And God saw that the light was good...

Genesis 1: 3-4

Many of us may be guilty of having a skewed understanding of success. We think that it's a single moment in time when we can show the world our amazing gifts and how much we've prepared for a certain event. But success is more than a star athlete winning the championship game or a student passing their last exam to earn a diploma, certificate, or degree. Success is a series of seemingly small steps that collectively have great impact. Success is diligently preparing for whatever opportunity presents itself. As you're working towards your goals, remember that you don't need to accomplish everything today. Doing a single thing that moves you closer to what you are trying to achieve is more than sufficient. And, always celebrate the small things; because big things are simply a series of small things.

Today I'm thankful that what seemed to be failures weren't final.
These things were lessons for and steppingstones to my success. Be encouraged and keep going.

DAY 25

IT'S OKAY

Since God chose you to be the holy people he loves, you must clothe yourselves with tenderhearted mercy, kindness, humility, gentleness, and patience. Make allowance for each other's faults, and forgive anyone who offends you. Remember, the Lord forgave you, so you must forgive others. Above all, clothe yourselves with love, which binds us all together in perfect harmony. And let the peace that comes from Christ rule in your hearts. For as members of one body you are called to live in peace. And always be thankful.

Colossians 3: 12-15

The pressure to perform is overwhelming. For many of us, we have been conditioned to believe that we must earn our way into others' good graces. And if we have to earn our way in, we also worry about doing something that will cause people to be disappointed in us and eventually change how they feel about us. It's unhealthy and exhausting. Today, think about how you can continually become a more accepting, more patient, and less judgmental sibling, spouse, friend, student, coworker, or neighbor. Because people already know when they have done something wrong, they don't need to be reminded of their missteps, mishaps, and mistakes. Instead they need to be supported as they endeavor to do better. Be encouraged and encourage someone else.

Today I am thankful for God's grace that says it's okay. In other words, despite what I've done,
It's okay = I'm not upset at you and I still love you.

DAY 26

GOD RESTORES THROUGH REST

The LORD is my shepherd; I have all that I need.
He lets me rest in green meadows; he leads me beside the peaceful streams.
He renews my strength...

Psalm 23: 1-3

Rest is essential to a healthy life. When cultures are preoccupied with business and busyness, rest can seem both counterintuitive and counterproductive. But not only is rest necessary, it's ordained by God. The physical body's way of replenishing and repairing itself, rest also rejuvenates the soul. Rest is so important that a few moments of peace and quiet can improve our moods, clear our minds, and enable us to function more effectively. Today, and every day, give yourself a break by taking a break. And despite what you might have been taught, you don't always have to earn it; you deserve it.

There is a quiet place far from the rapid pace
Where God can soothe my troubled mind
Sheltered by tree and flower there in my quiet hour
With him my cares are left behind
Whether a garden small, or on a mountain tall
New strength and courage there I find
And then from that quiet place I go prepared to face
A new day with love for all mankind[6]

---

[6]   Carmichael, Ralph. "A Quiet Place." *Take 6,* Reprise Records, 1988.

Today I'm grateful that God never rejects me but always accepts me. And despite my many missteps, God continually restores me. What are you grateful for today?

INCLUSION IS
MEANINGFUL PARTICIPATION

Just as our bodies have many parts and each part has a special function, so it is with Christ's body.
We are many parts of one body, and we all belong to each other.

Romans 12: 4-5

Inclusion is meaningful participation. It's diverse or different people being in the same group but each one feeling welcomed and having an opportunity to contribute to whatever is happening. In some ways, a puzzle is an appropriate metaphor for inclusion. Not only does each piece fit, but each piece also plays a significant role in the picture as a whole. And without each piece being in its rightful place, it's impossible for the picture to be complete. In the family of God, you are an intricate and necessary piece of the puzzle. And without you, the family wouldn't be the same—it would be incomplete.

Today I am grateful that God doesn't just accept me, but God fully includes me.
And more than being a friend of God, I am a part of the family of God.

DON'T WORRY

"That is why I tell you not to worry about everyday life—whether you have enough food and drink, or enough clothes to wear. Isn't life more than food, and your body more than clothing? Look at the birds. They don't plant or harvest or store food in barns, for your heavenly Father feeds them. And aren't you far more valuable to him than they are? Can all your worries add a single moment to your life? And why worry about clothing? Look at the lilies of the field and how they grow. They don't work or make their clothing, yet Solomon in all his glory was not dressed as beautifully as they are. And if God cares so wonderfully for wildflowers that are here today and thrown into the fire tomorrow, he will certainly care for you. Why do you have so little faith? So don't worry about these things, saying, What will we eat? What will we drink? What will we wear? These things dominate the thoughts of unbelievers, but your heavenly Father already knows all your needs."

Matthew 6: 25-32

Yes, it's easier said than done; but don't worry. Especially in moments of uncertainty, worry can quickly become fear and paralyzing anxiety. For those of us who may be worried about situations in our lives, it's not that worrying is wrong; it's just not helpful. In some ways, worry is a waste of valuable resources. As we're thinking about all of the negative things that could happen, precious time is being taken away from being productive. Worry also shifts our attention from what really matters: God's faithfulness to us. If you're like me and have worried about things in the past, was it helpful? Did worrying about what you didn't have or what you couldn't control help those situations? The answer is likely no. So instead of worrying, rest.

Today I am thankful that whatever I'm tempted to worry about, God has already figured out.

DAY 29

WHEN LATE IS RIGHT ON TIME

When Jesus arrived at Bethany, he was told that Lazarus had already been in his grave for four days. Bethany was only a few miles down the road from Jerusalem, and many of the people had come to console Martha and Mary in their loss. When Martha got word that Jesus was coming, she went to meet him. But Mary stayed in the house. Martha said to Jesus, "Lord, if only you had been here, my brother would not have died. But even now I know that God will give you whatever you ask." Jesus told her, "Your brother will rise again."

John 11: 17-23

It was early 1993 when I experienced it for the first time. My brothers and I wanted to attend a youth retreat with a national church organization. As we got closer to the date, my family still needed to pay for the trip. Although I was only 11 years old, I remember being in the basement of our home in Freeport, New York and this thought came to me: *God did not bring me this far to leave me.* I didn't know where the confidence came from, but I knew that we would have exactly what we needed. And as it worked out more than 27 years ago, it's happened for me on many occasions over the course of my life. Especially when it seemed as if it was too late, I have learned that it is impossible for God to be late. Why does God wait to make everything alright? While I can't speak for everyone, for me I believe it's God's way of making it clear that it was no one else but God. In the passage above, Jesus could have showed up earlier and prevented his friend from dying. But because he didn't arrive until Lazarus was dead for a few days, it was abundantly obvious that he was able to do the impossible. So, if God seems late in responding to you and your situation, remember that it's impossible for God to be late. What seems late to us is right on time for God.

Today, not only am I encouraged, but I'm also thankful that God's perfect timing paired with life's imperfections makes everything alright.

DAY 30

CELEBRATE LIFE

The faithful love of the LORD never ends! His mercies never cease.
Great is his faithfulness; his mercies begin afresh each morning.

Lamentations 3: 22-23

Released by The Winans in 1987, these lyrics are some of the most memorable of their decades-long career as well as Gospel music history: *millions didn't make it, but I was one of the ones who did.*[7] During a time in which a global pandemic has claimed the lives of close to 1 million people, this sentiment is particularly significant. Without a doubt, those who succumbed to COVID-19 could never have predicted not being here today. And while we are saddened to have lost friends and loved ones, we are counted among those who made it. Despite what is happening around us, and all of the imperfections and inconveniences of the present day, we can be grateful for the gift of life. Wherever you are, celebrate life—not just today, but every day.

---

7   Winans, Marvin. "Millions." *Decisions,* Qwest Records, 1987.

*I'm grateful for another opportunity to be grateful. As you read this note, remember:
you have at least one thing for which you can be thankful. Life is a gift.*

DAY 31

FOOTBALL AND FRIENDSHIP

A friend is always loyal, and a brother is born to help in time of need.

Proverbs 17: 17

Sometimes I wonder if our everyday language is too casual. The word love describes the deep affection that we have for our spouses and children as well as how we feel about our favorite foods and television shows. Similarly, the word friend seems to be overused. When we refer to others as our friends, what do we mean? I've learned that genuine friends are a rare commodity because true friendship is sacrificial. Like love, strong friendships develop over time and are demonstrated in life's most difficult and lonely circumstances. More than enjoying your company, friends sacrifice their comfort for your well-being. A friend blocks attacks that are coming your way. When others criticize you, a friend defends you. A friend doesn't cheer from the stands but joins you on the field and helps you score.

Like in football, sometimes God protects me by running alongside of me.
Today I am thankful that as I'm trying to move forward, God is in the struggle with me.

DAY 32

SECOND STEPS

For we live by believing and not by seeing.

2 Corinthians 5: 7

Have you ever had to walk in a dark room? What did you do? You likely carefully took one step, not knowing what you were going to step on or into. Was it comfortable? No. Was it scary? Yes. But you eventually made it to where you wanted to be. Much of life is similar to walking in dark places. We don't always know what's ahead of us or around us; but as we take one step, God orders our second steps. Will we stumble? Sometimes. Will we fall? Perhaps. But most times we land on our feet, which encourages us to keep going. God never expects us to know the way. Only God knows the end from the beginning. Instead, God wants us to have enough faith to take first steps, even small ones. And when we do, God will reveal all of our second steps.

Do you know what I am thankful for today?
That God never expects me to have everything figured out.
As I take one step, God will direct all of my second steps.

WHAT HAPPENED TO YOU?

"Do not judge others, and you will not be judged. For you will be treated as you treat others.
The standard you use in judging is the standard by which you will be judged.
And why worry about a speck in your friend's eye when you have a log in your own?"

Matthew 7: 1-3

Life teaches us to be more compassionate, more patient, and more understanding. Having said that I would never do certain things, and finding myself in those situations, I've also learned to never say never. Although it's easier to see the faults of others more than our own, we can do better. Consider this approach from an area of psychology. When people (e.g., children) are engaging in maladaptive behaviors, trauma-informed or trauma sensitive practices ask *what happened to you?* instead of *what's wrong with you?* By simply reframing the question, we shift the focus from the individual to circumstances that are often beyond their control. Because everyone is struggling with something, let's listen to others' stories and be more sensitive to what they've experienced in life.

I'm thankful that life teaches me not to judge anyone.
Loneliness can lead people to things they thought they'd never do.
If that's you, I am praying for you.

FROM DANGERS SEEN AND UNSEEN

I look up to the mountains—does my help come from there? My help comes from the LORD, who made heaven and earth! He will not let you stumble; the one who watches over you will not slumber. Indeed, he who watches over Israel never slumbers or sleeps. The LORD himself watches over you! The LORD stands beside you as your protective shade. The sun will not harm you by day, nor the moon at night. The LORD keeps you from all harm and watches over your life. The LORD keeps watch over you as you come and go, both now and forever.

Psalm 121

As a child, I often heard people say these words in their prayers: *protect us from dangers seen and unseen.* Although I had no idea what they were talking about, as I kept living it became clearer. Over time, I've also grown to be grateful for God's grace, which not only rescues us, but also proactively protects us from needing such intervention at all. In other words, grace as prevention shields us from dangers that we are aware of as well as those that we don't see coming our way. While God is strong enough to be the hero who intervenes on our behalf, God's divine protection is also powerful enough to prevent the need for intervention.

Just because it wasn't me, doesn't mean it couldn't have been me.
Today I'm grateful that grace continues to protect me from potentially devastating situations.

THE IRONY OF TRAFFIC

For you are my hiding place; you protect me from trouble...

Psalm 32: 7

Imagine traveling eastbound on a highway and there is bumper-to-bumper traffic in the opposite direction. As you continue driving, you realize that there are people going westbound but unaware of what's ahead of them. Whenever I see people speeding, only to be brought to a screeching halt, it strikes me as incredibly ironic. I want to warn them. I want to tell them to exit and go another way. Sometimes we are hastily heading somewhere, completely oblivious of what we're about to face. But God is always ahead of us. If we had left a few minutes earlier, we might have been involved in a terrible accident. Like someone traveling in the opposite direction, God has already been where we're going and has protected us from the destruction that we cannot see.

Today we can be thankful that the tragedies that could have happened did not happen.
Because God is always ahead of us, grace keeps us from what we cannot see.

I CAN DO IT MYSELF

Then he said, "I tell you the truth, unless you turn from your sins and become like little children, you will never get into the Kingdom of Heaven. So anyone who becomes as humble as this little child is the greatest in the Kingdom of Heaven."

Matthew 18: 3-4

Children have too many amazing qualities. Honest. Inquisitive. Innocent. Enthusiastic. Loving. Caring. And although they don't always admit it, children are also dependent. They innately know that they need help. They ask their parents to pick them up. They want to be held and carried. But as they grow, their quest for independence leads to, as one of my nephews used to say, *I can do it myself.* As we mature from children to adolescents, then young adults, and eventually adults, we must balance our need for healthy independence with recklessly abandoning those who know more than we do. Like little children, acknowledging that we need help is not a sign of weakness, but recognition that we are still growing. It's knowing that we don't know everything. It's having a teachable spirit—one that is receptive to the wisdom of those who have lived longer and know the way.

Because God is ahead of us, we don't have to know the way. Today we can be thankful that not going ahead of God, but following God, keeps us from getting lost.

IT WON'T ALWAYS BE LIKE THIS

*The LORD will work out his plans for my life—for your faithful love,
O LORD, endures forever. Don't abandon me, for you made me.*

Psalm 138: 8

Is hard work important? Yes. Is being diligent necessary to accomplish your goals? Yes. Is consistency central to success? Absolutely. These things, however, are difficult without hope. Today I want to encourage you: if you don't have anything else, hold on to hope. Hold on to the conviction that you are doing something that is helping your family, community, or even the world. Struggles will come your way, challenging moments are inevitable, and discouragement is a part of the process. But none of these things lasts forever. The small steps that you're taking to keep moving forward are bringing you closer to your expected end.

Today I am thankful that God never leaves anything incomplete.
And in the words of Psalm 138: 8, God will perfect (finish, fulfill) everything that concerns me.

DAY 38

YOU WILL FINISH

*And I am certain that God, who began the good work within you, will continue
his work until it is finally finished on the day when Christ Jesus returns.*

Philippians 1: 6

In May 2013 I completed my doctoral studies in school psychology. And like many others, the road to the PhD wasn't linear for me. In fact, it took 11 years. Life happens and what we intend doesn't always materialize as we originally planned. Yes, it's a bumpy and winding road; but hold on. Enjoy the ride. Remain focused on completing that which you've started. You'll make it. One day at a time. You'll finish. The cloud over your head will go away, life is sweeter on the other side, and it will be worth it.

Because God never leaves anything unfinished, if I'm alive, there must be more for me to accomplish. Today I'm thankful that my life is synonymous with purpose.

DAY 39

IN MY ROOM

O God, listen to my cry! Hear my prayer! From the ends of the earth, I cry to you for help when my heart is overwhelmed. Lead me to the towering rock of safety, for you are my safe refuge, a fortress where my enemies cannot reach me.

Psalm 61: 1-3

The lyrics below are taken from the 1963 release of *In My Room,* a timeless ballad by the Beach Boys. In recent years, public schools have created calm areas for children who become overwhelmed. Often having pillows and blankets, dim lighting, books, and sometimes soft music, it's a space where they can process their feelings and collect themselves before rejoining their peers. Like children, we also need a safe space. A place of quiet rest. A place that's away from life's noisy distractions. A place of peace. A place to think. A place to gather strength. A place to pray. And, a place to listen. Where is your safe space?

There's a world where I can go and tell my secrets to

In my room, in my room

In this world I lock out all my worries and my fears

In my room, in my room[8]

As children deserve a peaceful space when they are feeling overwhelmed,
we also need a place of quiet rest. What are you thankful for today?

DAY 40

REFLECT

*"We will use these stones to build a memorial. In the future your children will ask you, 'What do these stones mean?' Then you can tell them, 'They remind us that the Jordan River stopped flowing when the Ark of the LORD's Covenant went across.'
The stones will stand as a memorial among the people of Israel forever."*

Joshua 4: 6-7

I earned my undergraduate degrees in English and psychology from St. John's University. A Catholic institution, students were required to take courses in religion and philosophy. During this time, I was exposed to Rene Descartes, a French philosopher, mathematician, and scientist. One of his most famous statements is *Cogito, ergo sum*, a Latin phrase that essentially means *I think, therefore I am*. Coupled with that assertion, he wrote *A Thinking Thing*. Taken together, one of the defining features of human existence is the ability to think and reason. And having the capacity to think, we can reflect on the many blessings that God has bestowed upon us. Although they are too numerous to name, the intentionality of thinking is nonetheless meaningful. Even when we can't recall everything, it's always good to reflect. In fact, it's the sentiment that's captured in Count Your Blessings[9]: purposefully thinking about and reflecting upon what God has done for us. As counting is a deliberate action, so is thanksgiving.

---

9   Oatman, Johnson. (1897). *Count Your Blessings.*

*Instead of counting my blessings, I will spend time reflecting on and remembering them—
not just today, but all year long. Every day is a day of thanksgiving.*

Made in USA - Kendallville, IN
1181518_9781735026411
10.16.2020 0808